scorpio

october 23 • november 22

WHITE STAR PUBLISHERS

contents

Character and Temperament 4

Love and Passion 8

How to Hook a Scorpio and How to Let Them Go 12

Compatibility with Other Signs 14

Scorpio Profession and Career 16

How Scorpio Thinks and Reasons 20

Sociability, Communication and Friendship 24

Text by
Patrizia Troni

Graphic Design
Maria Cucchi

When Scorpio Gets Angry 28

Scorpio Children 30

Music Associated with Scorpio 32

Colors Associated with Scorpio 34

Flowers and Plants Associated with Scorpio 36

Animals Associated with Scorpio 38

Gemstones Associated with Scorpio 40

Best Food for Scorpio 42

Myths Associated with Scorpio 44

Scorpio Fairy Tale 46

Character and Temperament

Scorpio is considered one of the strongest and most combative signs in the entire Zodiac. Scorpio has a reputation for being an inexhaustible, unwavering, audacious and indestructible warrior because they have been blessed with an exceptional sniper scope of the subconscious that allows them to focus on anything that moves, even in the dark.

Scorpio is astute, profound, silent, lethal and intelligent, marked by a very slow pace that often comes to a halt, ready to spring at their prey at the opportune moment. They are true warriors who never lose their concentration and focus. They not only have two eyes at the front, but others behind and at the side as well. They do not content themselves with what apparent reality shows them, since they know, as Heraclitus said, that the truth lies in what is hidden. They disregard the mere form and superficiality of existence and go straight to the substance. Their eyes penetrate into the soul of others, even into the darkest recesses. They are the strength of the body and, in particular of the psyche. They are powerful, and filled with inexhaustible energy.

Their restless and tormented nature, their compulsion to be always vigilant, just like a warrior, on the lookout for anything that moves in the dark, is also reflected back on themselves; it also acts within them, like some never-ending tension that, at times, may turn into torture. Warriors never rest, warriors never make themselves comfortable, they never stop practicing their sword craft even without a real enemy.

Their temperament is really quite simple. On the one hand, there is unwavering, boundless, explosive energy that cannot remain static but always seems to be on the verge of erupting and becoming a tsunami. And, on the other hand, there is an intelligent, intuitive and very lucid mind that wants and expects to govern this extraordinary energy and keep it under control. The upshot is an inner conflict in which the soul can never be at peace because its function as a controlling agent cannot allow this energy to flow freely as merely unconscious instinct. They must understand everything, possess everything, and be stronger than the dynamite that is inside them. Thus, we have an endless inner conflict with a tendency toward self-punishment and self-sacrifice, because a warrior must constantly train in order be prepared for all eventualities.

Another Scorpio characteristic that must be mentioned is their nomadic nature, the urge to leave a 'settled' and known territory and venture into uncharted lands, because, for Scorpio, life means endless movement and, above all, knowledge, since knowledge is something that never ends and has no limits. This is partly why they are unable to accept tranquility; once attained, it becomes bothersome and intolerable. Life must be restlessness, quest, investigation, conquest. As Hegel stated, restlessness is the Self. They are dialectic, occasionally provocative war machines that put others through their paces. They seek the limit, the barrier, because they like to challenge themselves and demonstrate to themselves that nothing and no one can keep them within bounds. And, should someone attempt to put them in a circle of impassable fire one day and they were to find that they were enclosed and limited, then, like a scorpion, they would raise their black tail ready to exact revenge. A great warrior can never be captured. A great warrior, wrapped in blue veils, moves on in the desert like a Tuareg, toward the infinite – with his magnetism, his remarkable fascination, his impenetrable aura of mystery.

Love and Passion

8 Scorpio

Scorpio is remarkably passionate, but this emotion is not limited to sentimental poetry and romantic walks hand in hand in the moonlight. No, for Scorpio, love means giving everything and demanding everything, often bordering on the riskiest and most electrifying territories to which they may be led by overpowering desire. Scorpio is, undoubtedly, one of the most erotic signs of the Zodiac, if not the most erotic, and this reputation is certainly merited. But, for Scorpio, sex and desire are not natural and immediate, limited to the pleasure of the flesh and mere physical sexuality. Love, passion and eroticism always take on a highly cerebral overtone that seems to be in contradiction with mere physical satisfaction. Love and eroticism become a thrilling game of subtle, uninterrupted, lucid and rational strategy, much like a game of chess in which one can directly attack the king or queen; but this conquest must be prepared by means of outflanking moves that, slowly but surely, push the object of their desire into a corner.

Their remarkable intuition and telepathic gift make it possible for them to perceive everything from and about their partner, to grasp their innermost essence and thoughts. Their greatest pleasure is not to

manifest their love openly, but to play on silence and rapid, nearly imperceptible glances that penetrate the other person like a gamma ray. They handle love at a distance, they see it without looking at it, arouse it without coming very near. Hence, it becomes a sensational crescendo that is more overwhelming and intriguing the longer they are able to wait for fulfillment of their desire. This is why they are masters of eroticism, because they do not give in immediately to the imperative voice of romance.

In matters of love, they not only want to dominate and possess the other person, sometimes even placing them in a vice-like grip much like the most exciting forms of torture, but, above all, they want to dominate and totally control themselves, they want to demonstrate that they can do this and that nothing and no one is able to get them so carried away that they lose their self-control and rationality.

But, this inner torment is not something that ends up in total immobility. It is a means of increasing passion to excess. And, when it explodes – because it will certainly explode eventually – it is of the greatest intensity, a most powerful vibration that, at one fell swoop, involves the body, the mind and even the soul.

Being in love with Scorpio entails taking part in a game it will be difficult to pull out of lightly and nonchalantly. Being in love with Scorpio is rather like entering an extraordinarily attractive labyrinth, from which one part of the other person would like to escape in order to find a more peaceful and serene relationship, but another part cannot do this because it is bewitched by a spell it cannot do without anymore and can no longer escape from. This does not mean that Scorpio is unable to create a profound, eternal, indissoluble love with a partner. Besides being strong and able to resist the above-mentioned intensity of passion, their partner must know how to create an intelligent, and, above all, confident, relationship.

When Scorpio loves another Scorpio, they will love them forever. When they fall in love, when they have decided to overcome all complications and resistance, when they have taken the step – then they become a partner who is an immense bulwark and force in the life of the couple. And, all that destabilizing, erotic energy they used in seducing their lover is now transformed into a trustworthy and very profound sentiment that loves with a persistence, and an intelligence, that is perhaps unequalled.

How to Hook a Scorpio and How to Let Them Go

Scorpio is a mysterious creature. Like a matryoshka doll, every day they reveal a new side of their character. It is not always easy to love them, and hooking them is a feat that requires energy, presence of mind, vigilance and a truly passionate heart. The reward, their love, is something that is powerful and magical, both sweet and bitter, romantic and destructive, serene and contentious. A love that, for the other person, is a casket full of surprises, not suitable for the weak who are as soft as cheese spread. They need someone who, once having decided to share their life with you, does not back off but goes all the way.

The vamp, the malicious and seductive femme fatale, is the type that will most likely impress the Scorpio male. The secret lies in the following: high heels, garters, provocative but not vulgar lingerie, and a total lack of submissiveness. The Scorpio male does not like easy conquests. He wants a strong woman who can hold her own and who disappears every once in a while, planting suspicion in his mind. A woman who never makes him feel totally sure of himself but who, however, is always present and with great patience tolerates his mental contortions and covert anguish. In order to conquer the Scorpio female one must bear in mind that she is like Mata Hari, a dark lady with great seductive power. If she has an affair with a weak man, she makes him her slave but soon tires of him. She wants a man with a strong, determined, erotically imaginative personality. A man who courts her slowly, progressively, and then suddenly overwhelms her. One who is not morbidly jealous but whose suspicion and mistrust clearly reveals how much he wants her. Before breaking a relationship with Scorpio, it is best to prepare an escape route, because their vengefulness is proverbial. In order to leave them, you must tell them outright that you have no more feelings for them and then hope for the best – that is, that they will believe you.

Compatibility with Other Signs

The most profound elective affinities, most intriguing games of seduction and eroticism that is truly breathtaking, can be experienced with others who have the same Water element. They will find areas of high-level sensuality, sensitivity, attention and perceptive capabilities in Cancer or Pisces. A relationship with Taurus is a question of love and hate, Eros and Thanatos, war and peace. Each desires the other, likes the other, are mutually attracted and jealous, and each irritates the other. There are differences of opinion, especially concerning how to manage the family budget, spiteful acts due to jealousy, as well as possessiveness, which is latent in both signs. With Aquarius, there is a strong feeling of attraction and empathy, but with its ups and downs. When things are going well Scorpio comes close to paradise; but when things are going badly Scorpio is involved in pitiful emotional blackmail, disappearances and re-appearances that risk poisoning the relationship. The competitive spirit of Aries and Leo, in the professional sphere, create incompatibility and differences of opinion. With these signs, the art of compromise must be active in order to sustain agreement and love. There is compatibility based on logic with Gemini and Virgo, which are perfect signs for business, alliances and friendship. Scorpio likes the tranquil nature of Virgo because they adore upsetting their rational and balanced world, and they like being upset in return. They like Sagittarius because of the energy, but their straightforward behavior does not always agree with the Machiavellian mind of Scorpio. The couple functions better in work relations and friendship than in the romantic sphere. Capricorn is ambitious and wants to dominate, just like Scorpio, so that great understanding and fellowship can be established, and together they can elevate the world. But, should there be disagreement, then it is war with no holds barred. Lastly, with another Scorpio it is 'love at first bite', vampiric love, overwhelming, profound, wildly enthusiastic and total. Their relationship consists of intoxicating sex as well as a veritable roller coaster of mutual suspicion and distrust, torment, accusation and apology.

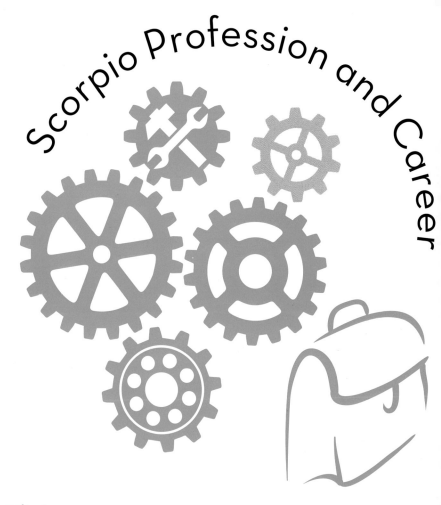

Scorpio Profession and Career

Scorpio is ruled by Mars, the planet of tenacity and forcefulness. When this aggressive quality is applied to the work world Scorpio demonstrates unusual determination, obstinacy, and stamina. No effort, however great, frightens them; on the contrary, they like toil and struggle, they adore surpassing their limits and they combine this quality with great tactical and strategic intelligence.

Silently, they work their way up their career ladder. They plan and, inevitably, make progress, advance in rank, in general alternating moments of carefully and rationally measured and muffled steps with other moments in which they take risks and gamble, and even probe the unknown, in their job.

They alternate the spirit of a great politician, who loves to move his pawns skillfully and stealthily, with the spirit of a great entrepreneur, who loves complex undertakings and difficult challenges, because the word 'impossible' does not exist for Scorpio. In fact, there are many business executives born under Scorpio who take over a company in serious trouble and then successfully put it back on its feet. They are attracted by difficulty. They were not born for dull, routine jobs in which they are only waiting for payday to arrive. Work, like life itself for that matter, must be an exciting form of combat, and even the world of finance, with all the risk it entails, attracts Scorpio. And, when they have accumulated some capital, they prefer to risk it, thus facing a new challenge. This is the reason why Scorpio has so many financial wizards and leading entrepreneurs. But, even on a lower, more common level, in a normal office, they are the ones who cannot be idle and, above all, cannot stop using their lively mind. They want a lively, dynamic profession in which challenges alternate with intelligent and opportunistic calculation.

Sometimes impassible, sometimes explosive, in a work team they are the spearhead who penetrates, the energy and strength that is transmitted to all their colleagues. They immediately see a problem for what it is, and like to face it and solve it; they know how to evaluate the worst scenario, which is their great virtue, and they never let themselves be carried away by silly optimism. They can be self-disciplined and postpone doing something if it is not the opportune moment, because they always have the objective clearly in mind and never give in until it has been achieved. They are astute and ironic, which helps them in work relationships because others listen to them and appreciate their opinions.

In some cases, this astuteness may also mean being calculating. Indeed, they can go one better than the devil himself. They are shrewd, always able to perceive the most hidden side of the personality of their clients, competitors, colleagues, superiors and subordinates. This capacity to penetrate the unconscious of others is a great help in attaining a result, and such close relationship with the hidden aspects of others' natures has led many a Scorpio to become psychoanalysts and psychiatrists. They can see way beyond the limits of normal eyesight. Thanks to this bond with the subterranean and with secrets, and their passion for the mysterious, there are many Scorpio spies and secret agents, criminologists and infallible private and police investigators. They are invincible lawyers because they know how to find their opponents' weak point and to win cases with syllogisms and sophisms. They are directors who love to lead without exposing themselves. Even when they are sometimes restless and impulsive, they always keep a sense of perspective regarding the objective. And, they have the strength to start over again. The fact that Scorpio is associated with what is under the earth's surface has produced speleologists, oil magnates, and others whose professions are connected with the subterranean.

How Scorpio Thinks and Reasons

The attribute most suited to Scorpio intelligence is profundity. Their intelligence is not quick, the kind that, in an instant, is able to gather many different data, but is superficial and limited to an evaluation of the exterior effects of a situation. And, one could not even state that theirs is the type of intelligence that confines itself to analyzing concrete facts, an analytical and literal mode of reasoning that views things just as they are.

No, their intelligence heads straight to the cause of things, what lies behind the effects and behind appearances. Therefore, they go to the heart of the matter and the truth, they aim right at the essence that is the source of all forms, words and actions.

It is a question of profundity, the ability to see inside, to penetrate, with two fine instruments: relentless reasoning combined with formidable intuition. Their mind does not allow itself to be enchanted by forms or facile enthusiasm. They remain cold and grasp things slowly, arriving at the heart of the matter stubbornly and patiently, partly thanks to their uncommon power of observation. They see without being seen, which gives them an advantage over others.

They are suspicious of those who claim they understand everything in an instant. Although their power of observation seldom fails them, they do not trust that 'first glance'. They examine and re-examine their hypothesis, as if the truth were prey that must be stalked slowly and, once captured, never be allowed to escape.

Their judgment or opinion is always carefully prepared, after a rather tormented and tortuous process, but when they finally give their opinion, it is irrevocable.

They are the masters of shadow, obscurity, and the hidden. For Scorpio, what must truly be understood is always lying hidden in dark recesses. They like to probe, investigate, and slowly discover things. Mystery and the unknown attract and fascinate them, and in their opinion, there is very little in life that is superficial. The banal truths, those taken for granted, and the routine mode of reasoning that proceeds only by means of clichés, irritate them immensely. They have too much respect for human intelligence to like those who do not want to reflect, who take everything for granted, and who only want to show how much they know. They dislike know-it-alls, erudite people who show off their 'culture' as an end in itself, the vain who always want to be the center of attention. And, although they adore people with a wealth of emotions, they have no intention whatsoever of being blinded by emotion. For Scorpio, mental lucidity is something that must never go astray, and not even the strongest sentiment must go so far as to cloud and befog one's intelligence.

Sometimes, this intelligence becomes sheer torture, because their mind never stops considering, reflecting, and viewing things from all angles. But, it is precisely this style that makes their brain one of the most subtle and extraordinary in the Zodiac.

However, from time to time, it wouldn't be a bad idea for them to try to understand with a more relaxed, softer approach, to stop mistrusting their natural instincts and trust more in sensations, because in life it is not always necessary that the mental prevails over the emotional. Their exceptional intelligence often ends up paralyzing and blocking them. Instead of releasing their energy, they allow it to accumulate inside, which will, eventually, lead to an explosion. While it is true that the deepest truth is the one with the most quality, it is also true that the beauty of life can be expressed in a somewhat carefree and ingenuous manner.

Sociability, Communicatior

and Friendship

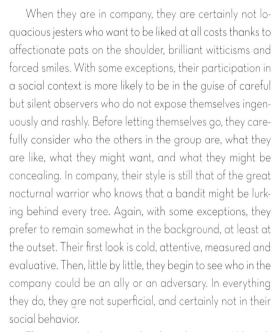

When they are in company, they are certainly not loquacious jesters who want to be liked at all costs thanks to affectionate pats on the shoulder, brilliant witticisms and forced smiles. With some exceptions, their participation in a social context is more likely to be in the guise of careful but silent observers who do not expose themselves ingenuously and rashly. Before letting themselves go, they carefully consider who the others in the group are, what they are like, what they might want, and what they might be concealing. In company, their style is still that of the great nocturnal warrior who knows that a bandit might be lurking behind every tree. Again, with some exceptions, they prefer to remain somewhat in the background, at least at the outset. Their first look is cold, attentive, measured and evaluative. Then, little by little, they begin to see who in the company could be an ally or an adversary. In everything they do, they are not superficial, and certainly not in their social behavior.

This approach does not last long, however. Although they are people of few words, their sense of irony is eloquent. And, should they not like the person(s) they are talking to, this irony can become sarcastic or even vitriolic.

But, where friendship is concerned, their friends know that they can count on them totally. They can keep a secret and avoid saying what must not be said. Words do not flow from their mouth loosely, and, in conversation, they are never too hasty or impulsive. Furthermore, they are excellent listeners who not only analyze conversations and acts, but also observe what lies behind them. They have the gift of being able to penetrate others' subconscious and discern the most mysterious and recondite recesses of the human soul. When a person has become a very good friend, they put their exceptional strength at the other's complete disposal. They are faithful in true friendship, but this does not imply that they are ingenuous. Should someone betray their friendship, then their spirit of vendetta is notorious, and it can be carried out much later, when the other least expects it. In short, it is much better to be their friend than their enemy.

In any case, they know how to evaluate people's hearts, and when the heart of another proves to be pure and sincere, they become the most precious of friends, those one can count on, especially at crucial moments. While others are waving the white flag of surrender, Scorpio still has a reserve of energy left. And, when the going gets tough, it is tough persons like Scorpio who take action.

People say it is not easy to get along with a Scorpio, which is sometimes true, of course. But, it is also true that they are always interesting, never banal and dull, and when they feel comfortable in a social context they become a positive force at everyone's disposal.

In a group, in company or in a team they are not a conceited, show-off leader who wants to hog the limelight at all costs, but when a very important decision must be made, all eyes are focused on them. They need only utter a few words to make themselves clear and those who are pursuing the same objective soon become familiar with their tenacity and determination, their boundless passion, that bold and courageous subversive energy that takes risks and is an indispensable asset for the group.

Naturally, they can also be light-hearted and entertaining, cheerful and likeable. And, the exceptional quality of their irony allows them to utter fundamental truths with a simple comment. They can make people smile but they can also make them think. No one could ever accuse Scorpio of being stupid or shallow.

When Scorpio Gets Angry

Their fits of anger arrive like a raging torrent. They flow underground and then suddenly erupt. Scorpio anger rises slowly, like magma in a volcano, and when it explodes, it overwhelms everything with a spectacular show. They use their tail to kill their prey, and they annihilate others with words that cut like a sword made of Toledo steel and with the power of caustic logic. There are two kinds of anger in their repertoire. There is the type that develops slowly until it flares up, catching the other person by surprise, and immediate anger, characterized by its impressive violence and its dangerously destructive potential. When Scorpio gets angry then the sky's the limit, nothing and no one can stop them, and they are afraid of nothing. They go into battle and fight to the bitter end. They do not back away or mediate. Either, they win or they lose. In the Scorpio DNA, there is no such thing as a middle way: it's either black or white, either they are right or they are wrong. But, if they are right, then they go the whole hog. Scorpio rage is proverbial because it puts others with their backs against the wall and with no possibility of escape.

But, who is that makes them angry? Those who take them for a weakling and think they can easily take advantage of them and treat them arrogantly and in a patronizing manner. Scorpio is a sign of great political skill; with their intelligence they can map out strategies, find allies, accomplices and friends. But, diplomacy goes out the window if someone provokes them. When faced with stupid, banal, vulgar, or mean types then there are no half measures. Scorpio becomes more deadly than the Terminator. By nature, they are discreet. For Scorpio, a secret is strictly personal and private. If they confide in someone, it is because they trust that person totally. But, if someone betrays their trust then this will trigger cold anger that that person will find difficult, if not impossible, to placate.

Scorpio Children

Dynamic, strong-willed, and combative, Scorpio children have a determined and latently unmanageable personality. From a very early age, they manifest great self-esteem and they expect others to be the same. This does not make them a time bomb ready to explode or a miniature Attila. One should not think of them as irritable or disobedient, and difficult to control.

Their parents should not oppose or try to thwart their strong temperament, their love of challenges and provocation, but should channel these inclinations intelligently, gently and constructively. If they are misunderstood, not guided or loved, their critical nature may become rebellious, obstinate, and resistant to punishment. But, if they are understood and followed, these little warriors will develop strength of character, and an indomitable determination that will be very useful in their adult life.

Their acute intelligence, critical and cool way of looking at things, and desecrating irony make them attentive and precise observers. This means that their parents' faults, and certain illogical scolding and prohibitions, will not pass unseen or be easily forgotten.

They may do well at school but, often, they work hard only if the subject or the teacher fascinates and interests them. Otherwise, they are quite content to have average grades – not because they are not competitive, but because they do not waste their energy or their intelligence on what they find uninteresting.

In general, they prefer older playmates, but they are quite happy to be alone, because they are not the type who get bored if they have no one to play with. They tend to be very protective of smaller children.

Their extremely lively intelligence should be stimulated from an early age with formative games.

Music Associated

Musical style is rich, meaty, vigorous and powerful, in Scorpio. This can be seen in such extraordinary Scorpio composers as Domenico Scarlatti and Vincenzo Bellini. Scorpio music alternates power and sudden flashes of poetry, lyricism and moments of great breadth, exemplified by Johann Strauss, Georges Bizet or the great violin virtuoso Niccolò Paganini, who could not have been more Scorpio than when he played Tartini's *The Devil's Trill* sonata. Scorpio music can also be theatrical. It transmits great emotional intensity that very skillfully plays on suspense, as if its sound always evokes other sounds, other possibilities, or other infinite variations.

Scorpio is not the type of composer who overloads their compositions. Their music is exceptional in its play on pauses and silence, as in the case of Ennio Morricone's film scores or the refined and avant-garde atmosphere created by Luciano Berio.

As stage performers, instead of a sunny, extrovert image they prefer a persona that is vigorous and powerful, yet with a touch of the mysterious - hard and tough, as, for

with Scorpio

example, Simon Le Bon of Duran Duran, or with sudden spurts of magic and poetic atmosphere, as is the case with Bryan Adams.

The public persona of Scorpio singers must always contain something provocative, as if the music and its interpretation always has to throw down the gauntlet and challenge the whole world, even transmitting a powerful and rebellious image of themselves, as is the case with American singer Katy Perry, whose magnetic eyes are totally Scorpio, as is her hit *Dark Horse*. If there were an instrument, in the Zodiac orchestra, that could be associated with Scorpio, then it would be the electric bass or contrabass guitar. This is because, like the contrabass, Scorpio does not always like to be in the limelight, but prefers to be the robust backbeat that sustains the entire rhythmical structure.

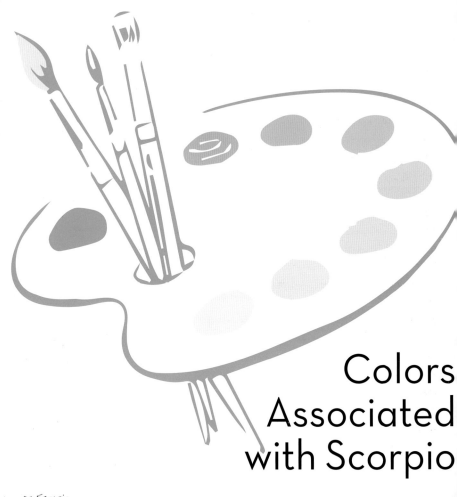

Colors
Associated
with Scorpio

Black is the color of Scorpio, the color that conceals, masks, annuls all the other colors. The black of darkness, of an obscure abyss, of Hell. It is the color that most reflects their subversive and instinctive spirit; their fondness for the macabre, for drama; the theatrical, dominant, rebellious side of their nature. In the Western world, black is the color of mourning, while for Asians mourning is expressed with the color white and for the ancient Romans it was gray. It is the color of elegance (the Chanel little black dress) and impurity, of prohibition and authority (the black robes worn by magistrates, judges, priests, sport referees). It would almost seem that there are two blacks, one good and the other bad, just like the Scorpio character, which is sometimes torn between morality and vice, goodness and wickedness. It is easy to relate the black flag on pirate ships to their strong and determined side, their capacity to make a foray and take what they want, with force if necessary. But, black is also the color that waits on the sidelines and, like Scorpio, takes a back seat, while, at the same time, maintaining complete control. In ancient Rome, the Latin words *niger* stood for brilliant black and *ater* opaque black. Scorpio intelligence is among the most acute, meticulous, tormented and obscure in the Zodiac. Scorpio should choose brilliant black if they don't want their mind to lose its way but to go directly in search of a solution to problems, if they want to be lucid and able to focus on the target. This color will help them be impartial and dominate situations, and overturn them, if necessary. In their profession, and their love life, brilliant black provides inexhaustible, explosive, disruptive energy. Opaque black does not dull, but stimulates and brings to the fore their most attentive, circumspect and silent side. This color reconciles their mind and their instinct, their intelligence and their passion, and helps to choose allies, to understand what is advantageous for them and to put their heart in order.

Flowers
and Plants
Associated
with
Scorpio

Scorpio symbolizes the fallow period in the plant life cycle, the time when the land waits for spring to arrive. In fact, on October 31 and November 1 the Celts celebrated Samhain, the Celtic New Year, which marked the end of the harvest season and the beginning of winter. When the Sun is in Scorpio, the leaves fall, rot and become humus that fertilizes the earth. Scorpio is the sign of the inevitable end and death, death that germinates new life. The analogy with death associates Scorpio with such poisonous plants as hemlock, stinking hellebore, henbane, monk's hood and mandrake (a powerful and magical herb par excellence), as well as with carnivorous plants of the *Nepenthes* genus. Other flowers associated with Scorpio are the hydrangea, oleander, carnation, crocus and tamarisk.

The following are the flowers and the plants for each ten-day period.

First period (October 23-November 2): tuberose. Its white and very fragrant flowers make Scorpio seductive, tender, magical, sweet and very romantic. Given as a pledge of love, it can help to achieve success in transient love affairs.

Second period (November 3-12): asphodel. Homer considered this to be the flower of the underworld, while, for Epimenides of Knossos, it drove away hunger and lengthened one's lifespan. Considering it a plant with magical powers, Pliny advised people to plant it in front of their houses to ward off negative influences. Erasmus of Rotterdam wrote that where there is asphodel there is no folly. This flower keeps one far away from obsessive forms of jealousy and obsessive thoughts, and helps one to face and deal with everything.

Third period (November 13-22): mugwort. This plant was sacred to the god Mars and instills courage and determination. In the ancient world it was worn by wanderers because it was believed that it kept one's energy intact and that, if placed in one's shoes, relieved fatigue. Furthermore, it protected one from theft, lightning and the evil eye. Mugwort increases one's concentration and self-control, and recharges the batteries.

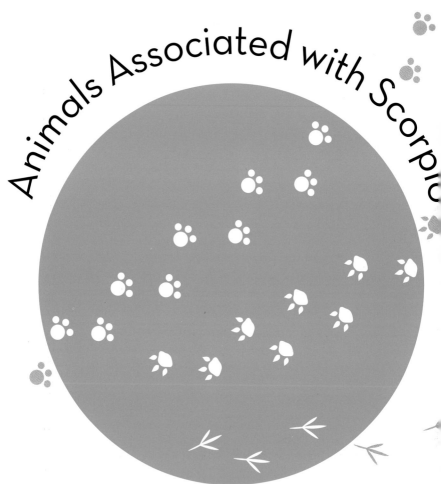

Animals Associated with Scorpio

Needless to say, the scorpion is the animal-symbol for this sign of the Zodiac. It is silent and its sting is lethal. Certain African tribes avoid even uttering the word 'scorpion', because its mention unleashes evil forces. But, among the Maya, the scorpion was a divinity, the god of hunting and the symbol of penitence and blood-letting. It was also sacred to the ancient Egyptians. In Greek mythology, a scorpion took revenge on the hunter Orion, who had offended the goddess Artemis, by stinging him on his heel, whereupon the grateful goddess took the creature to heaven and transformed it into a constellation. The scorpion embodies the Scorpio bellicose spirit, which one is rarely able to avoid, and their caustic irony, which is quite often deadly. The silkworm, which remains in the dark of its cocoon until it has metamorphosed from a pupa to a light butterfly, symbolizes the Scorpio need to hide, conceal their inner self and reveal only the surface, the outward appearance: their essence is much more profound than it seems to be. All nocturnal creatures, and those that sting, are also associated with Scorpio: moths, bats, lemurs, cats, hedgehogs, foxes, wolves and bears; and bees, bumblebees, wasps and mosquitoes. The exceptionally cold-blooded nature of Scorpio, associates them with reptiles, especially snakes such as the cobra, viper, black mamba and rattlesnake, as well as the gecko, which is a nocturnal reptile. "Remember the cosmic serpent Kundalini, symbol of their great sexual energy, and Uroboros, the snake that eats its own tail, symbol of cyclical regeneration and the capacity to make a new start, to overcome and recover from all defeats. Among birds associated with Scorpio are the buzzard, nocturnal raptors such as the barn owl, tawny owl and little owl, and the sparrow hawk and cormorant. The predatory shark, the dangerous piranha and the peaceful goldfish all symbolize the two-fold nature of Scorpio who likes to provoke and torment, but is not lacking in humility and tenderness."

Gemstones Associated with Scorpio

Scorpio is sheer volcanic energy lying behind an impassable mask. Obsidian, a volcanic glass, is perfect for Scorpio. It was much appreciated by pre-Columbian civilizations in Central and South America, as well as by the ancient Egyptians, who carved scarabs and magic seals on it. Its black color reflects and releases Scorpio energy. Among primitive cultures, shards of obsidian were used to make spear points, knives, and cutting implements, while the Aztecs used obsidian dust to cicatrize wounds. Scorpio is always ready for battle. Scorpio was born to attack, to strike, and to transfix. It is advisable not to have them as enemies because they do not relent or forget; they may wait for years, but eventually, they will strike. And, just as obsidian has the power to inflict wounds as well as to heal them, Scorpio is cutting and, at the same time, a miracle worker. If they put their great power at others' disposal then they will set them on their feet again, save and regenerate them. If they wear an obsidian jewel, it would be a good idea to carve symbols on it that are associated with Scorpio, such as a scorpion, Uroboros, etc. This stone should be worn on the hand or the right side of the body to display the side of their character that is available, calm and harmonious, and if they want to control their emotions. They should wear it on their left side if they want to show that they have the killer instinct in them, or if they wish to rebel, emerge, attack and win.

Onyx is also closely related to Scorpio, along with heliotrope, also known as bloodstone because its red inclusions resemble spots of blood. Scorpio should choose onyx when they are under pressure, when they must face an uphill struggle and when they want to find the right practical answer to resolve the situation. They should wear heliotrope when they want to be invisible, move underwater, so to speak, or to pull the strings without anyone knowing about it.

Best Food for Scorpio

Scorpio is a complex sign. There is Fire generated by Mars. There is the Water element (Scorpio is the third sign of Water). There is the profundity of the Earth and the world under the earth's surface symbolized by Pluto (Scorpio is ruled by Mars and Pluto).

In order to combine these three elements let us begin with a delicacy from the earth, truffles. The ancient Greek physician Galen of Pergamon wrote that truffles are very nutritious and can produce intense delight and voluptuousness. The poet Juvenal states that this tasty fruit of a fungus was born under an oak tree thanks to a thunderbolt hurled by Jupiter. The father of the gods was known to be a great seducer, so it was only natural that the ancients should connect the truffle with skillful lovemaking. To this day, it is said to have aphrodisiac and energy-inducing properties. According to tradition, Scorpio is the sign of strong sexual appetite, so they don't need to arouse sexual desire. But, all aphrodisiac food is associated with Scorpio and, consequently, could be included in their diet, to taste: ginseng, ginger, hot pepper, black pepper, oysters, avocado (especially excellent for men: in the Aztec language this fruit is called *ahuacate* or testicle) and almonds (rich in vitamin E, and an aphrodisiac, especially for the Scorpio female).

Among the aromatic herbs, Scorpio should use lemon verbena (*Aloysia citrodora*) for tisanes and infusions and to make jam, fruit salads and liqueurs, as well as for a pleasurable 'magic spell': in ancient times people believed that simply by rubbing verbena leaves on their hands and then touching their beloved's hands they could hook them. Apart from lemon verbena, other vegetables and herbs connected to Scorpio are onions, shallots, leeks, laurel and turnip.

The most sensitive, and receptive side, connected to the Water element, is associated with fish such as tuna, salmon, trout, cod and swordfish.

Myths
Associated
with Scorpio

There are three mythological figures associated with Scorpio: Pluto, the Phoenix and Nemesis.

Pluto was the brother of Zeus and Poseidon, and when dominion over the world was divided into three parts he was given the underworld, Hades, and all the wealth of minerals and seeds under the surface of the earth. A dark, stern god (one of his epithets was 'He who is unfamiliar with the smile'), but the tender husband of Persephone, Pluto symbolizes the obscure side of Scorpio. Scorpio is considered to be the most evil and dangerous sign in the Zodiac. But, they are subversive because they do not accept comfortable and convenient facts. They provoke and put everything to the test because they want to be absolutely sure of those around them, and they want see if others are as strong as they are. Their words contain a dash of sulfurous spite, not because they are infernal beings, but because they like to fight, and this is the reason why they trigger situations that involve their taste for challenge and competition.

Pluto connects them to another Scorpio symbolic reference - death. Everything that smacks of the macabre, the funereal, cemeteries and spiritualism, as well as noir literature and films, is associated with Scorpio. In general, Scorpio is not afraid of death and is also of great help and comfort when dealing with those who are gravely ill or those in mourning. Pluto is the lord of the underworld. But, he is also the king of fertility and prosperity because the treasures hidden in the earth are his: *Plouton*, the dispenser of riches, symbolizes the Scorpio nose for business. Whoever should entrust Scorpio with their money can be sure that they will make it bring in profit because they are born moneymakers, champion negotiators, gamblers who risk because they know they will win.

Since they are the most vengeful sign in the Zodiac they are associated with Nemesis, the goddess of justice who metes out divine retribution, and also with the Phoenix, the mythological bird who was reborn from the ashes. Scorpio will never die but they may fall, yet just when it seems that they are on their last legs they somehow bring out the best in themselves.

Scorpio's Fairy Tale

In *The Selfish Giant,* Oscar Wilde tells the story of a giant, who, returning home, found a lot of children playing in his garden. He was furious and drove them away, then built a wall to keep them out. Summer arrived, but in his garden it was still winter and nothing grew there. One day the giant heard the melodious call of a little bird. He went to the window and saw the trees in blossom and the children running on the grass. Spring had returned because the children had climbed through a hole in the wall and their joyful cries now filled the air. The giant deeply regretted his selfishness, told the children he meant no harm and invited them to play as much as they wanted. He also helped the smallest child climb up the branches of a tree, after which the boy thanked the giant by kissing him. From that day on, the children played in the giant's lovely garden, but the smallest one was no longer to be seen, which made the giant very sad. Finally, one day, when the giant was very old and weak, he saw the child. He ran happily to greet him, only to realize that the little one had wounds in his hands and feet. The child reassured him they were the wounds of Love and that, since the giant had allowed him to play there, he would now take the giant with him to play in his garden in Paradise. Like the giant, Scorpio is an individualist, reserved, a bit overbearing and wants to have control of situations and not depend on anyone else. And, in their own way, they play like children. Occasionally, they disappear and then reappear. Those who love them must know that their love is an ongoing trial and that they must not succumb to enigmatic silence and to the specter of abandonment. The giant changed from an egoist to a kind person, representing two sides of the Scorpio character: Scorpio is battle as well as infinite tenderness, harshness and goodness. They are capable of deceiving, tricking and lying, but they can also be silent, discreet, and can keep a secret even under torture. They are diabolical, but they have a very big heart.

PATRIZIA TRONI, trained at the school of Marco Pesatori, writes the astrology columns for Italian magazines *Marie Claire* and *Telepiù*. She has worked in the most important astrology magazines (*Astra, Sirio, Astrella, Minima Astrologica*), she has edited and written the astrology supplement of *TV Sorrisi e Canzoni* and *Chi* for years, and she is an expert not only in contemporary astrology, but also in Arab and Renaissance astrology.

Photo Credits
Archivio White Star pages 28, 34, 38; artizarus/123RF page 20 center; Cihan Demirok/123RF pages 1, 2, 3, 4, 14, 30, 48; Yvette Fain/123RF page 46; file404/123RF page 16 bottom; Olexandr Kovernik/123RF page 42; Valerii Matviienko/123RF pages 8, 12; murphy81/Shutterstock page 44; Igor Nazarenko/123RF page 40; Michalis Panagiotidis/123RF pages 20, 21; tribalium123/123RF page 16; Maria Zaynullina/123RF page 36

WHITE STAR PUBLISHERS

WS White Star Publishers® is a registered trademark property of De Agostini Libri S.p.A.

© 2015 De Agostini Libri S.p.A.
Via G. da Verrazano, 15 - 28100 Novara, Italy
www.whitestar.it - www.deagostini.it

Translation: Richard Pierce - Editing: Norman Gilligan

ISBN 978-88-544-0970-5
1 2 3 4 5 6   19 18 17 16 15

Printed in China